Smelly Old History

Tudor Odours

Mary Dobson

FRANKLIN PIERCE
COLLEGE LIBRARY
RINDGE, N.H. 03461

OXFORD UNIVERSITY PRESS

Oxford University Press, Great Clarendon Street, Oxford OX2 6DP

Oxford New York Athens Auckland Bangkok Bogotá Bombay
Buenos Aires Calcutta Cape Town Dar es Salaam Delhi
Florence Hong Kong Istanbul Karachi Kuala Lumpur
Madras Madrid Melbourne Mexico City Nairobi Paris
Singapore Taipei Tokyo Toronto

and associated companies in
Berlin Ibadan

Oxford is a trade mark of Oxford University Press

© Mary Dobson 1997

First Published 1997

  3 5 7 9 10 8 6 4 2

Artwork by Vince Reid and Martin Cottam
Photographs: Museum of London: 10, 24;
Royal Collection Enterprises: 27

CURR
DA
316
063
1997

All rights reserved. No part of this publication may be reproduced, stored in a retrieval system, or transmitted, in any form or by any means, without the prior permission in writing of Oxford University Press. Within the UK, exceptions are allowed in respect of any fair dealing for the purpose of research or private study, or criticism or review, as permitted under the Copyright, Designs, and Patents Act, 1988, or in the case of reprographic reproduction in accordance with the terms of the licences issued by the Copyright Licensing Agency. Enquiries concerning reproduction outside those terms and in other countries should be sent to the Rights Department, Oxford University Press, at the address above.

This book is sold subject to the condition that it shall not, by way of trade or otherwise, be lent, re-sold, hired out or otherwise circulated without the publisher's prior consent in any form of binding or cover other than that in which it is published and without a similar condition including this condition being imposed on the subsequent purchaser.

A CIP catalogue record for this book is available from the British Library

ISBN 0-19-910096-9

Printed in Great Britain

Contents

Scratch the scented panels
lightly with a fingernail
to release their smell.

A Sense of the Past ～

Life and death in Tudor times could be really foul. In the towns, the streets were foul. In the country, it often wasn't much better. It was hard for most people to keep clean. It didn't matter who you were – peasant or prince, you released your Tudor odours in all directions, and had to put up with everyone else's too. One sure way for traitors to avoid the revolting stenches was to have their head chopped off. But that meant smelling the terrible odours of the Tower of London as they took their last breath.

Anne Boleyn enjoys a final gasp of Tudor odours.

Of all the senses of the past, we often forget the sense of smell! This book takes you as close as possible to smelly old history. It's filled with Tudor odours for you to scratch and sniff – the awful and the aromatic (but mostly the awful).

The odorous Tudors came to power in 1485 and ruled until 1603, when the stinking Stuarts took over. Read on to discover just why they were such an odorous lot. To be fair, they did try to cover it up, with herbs and perfumes, and exotic substances brought from distant lands. They also tried to encourage their citizens to keep clean, by washing at least a few times a year.

A plague doctor, with mask and herbal wand.

TUDOR ODOURS

1485 Henry the Seventh arrived on the scene,
       In habit and hygiene he wasn't too clean.
       His people were lousy, they sweated and shook,
       Their foul Tudor odours will waft through this book.

1509 Henry the Eighth was the foulest of all,
       Not only his tum but his breath did appall.
       His wives – he had six – took one whiff of his sock,
       And instantly sensed they were in for a shock.

1547 Poor Edward the Sixth was sickly and pale,
       He sneezed and he vomited food rank and stale.

1553 As for Lady Jane Grey, she ruled only nine days –
       Her head was chopped off in the latest foul craze.

1553 Mary the First was stern and devout,
       Strong incense and odours she wafted about.
       She tried to revive the old Catholic plot
       By filling the air with the stench of burnt Prot.

1558 Elizabeth One tried hard to smell sweet
       By sloshing on scent from her nose to her feet.
       She even was given the first flushing loo,
       But in brushing her teeth she hadn't a clue.

1603 At last, Tudor odours finally went,
       And so Stuart stinks replaced their scent.
       Now new kings and rulers came to fame,
       But smelly old history was just the same!

How to get rid of your
stinks onto someone else.

The rotting heads of executed traitors
were hung on London Bridge as a
smelly warning to others.

Stinking Streets ⌒

T ake a deep breath, and imagine living with 15,000 other smelly Tudors in this city of Norwich. Your nostrils are bombarded with all kinds of unsavoury and fetid smells. The streets are overflowing with stinking filth; the open drains are a festering stream of murky mud; pig manure and cattle dung are piled up high and buzzing with flies. And if the risk of stepping in something really stinky is worrying you, try looking up above to sniff a whole lot worse.

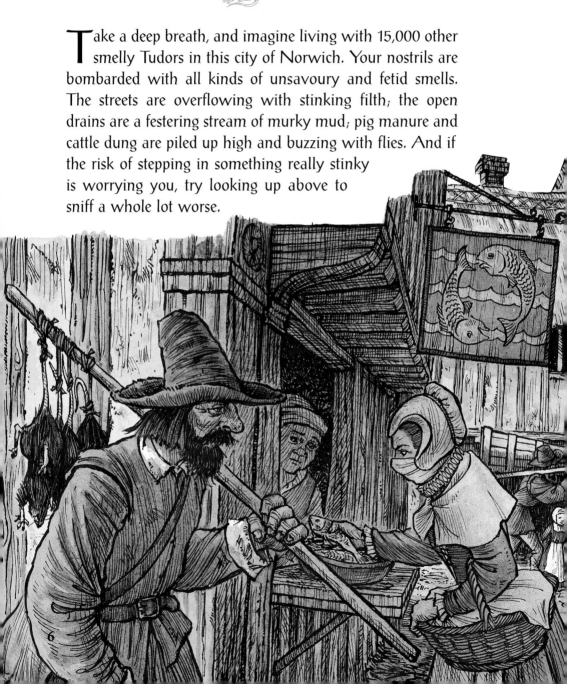

Dealing with all the awful smells and rotten rubbish was a problem that constantly plagued Tudor townsfolk. Indoor toilets hadn't been installed, and there were no proper drains. There was only one solution: to throw all the slops out onto the streets, and hope that the scavengers and rakers (two of the most odorous occupations of Tudor times) would shift it onto someone else's plot.

Scratch and sniff the rubbish for a truly Tudor odour.

Muck and Manure ~

Many people in Tudor times thought the natural smell of country air and thick farm manure was a lot better than the sickening stench of the town. This poor farmer is spreading dung on his small plot of land. His few animals and crops will supply his family with just enough to eat during the long, cold winter. He is proud to have a plot and not to have to beg or starve. Every season he patiently tills the soil, while his wife spins and weaves wool and his three children help to take the cloth to market. The good country air fills his lungs with well-being.

But inside his cottage, it's far from fragrant. On the floor are layers of rushes, each one festering with the previous year's rubbish. Spittle, dung, vomit, scraps of rotten meat, dead rats, animal offal – you name it, those rushes contain it.

Fortunately, these Tudor odours are rich in saltpetre, a substance which makes brilliant gunpowder. Every now and then the 'saltpetre men' charge into people's houses (often when they are asleep) and dig up their smelly floors, for making explosives for cannons and guns (now you know why we won the Armada).

Reeking Royals

Tudor kings and queens weren't just foul to other people – they were often pretty disgusting themselves. They couldn't really help it – with no proper sanitation or washing facilities they just had to hold their nose and bear it like the rest of the odorous Tudors.

Elizabeth I carried a pomander like this one. Each section contained a different smell, supposedly to ward off foul diseases. Even her gloves were scented, to perfume her regal little hands.

In 1485, after his victory at the battle of Bosworth during the Wars of the Roses (not a very fragrant event), Henry VII's coronation as the first Tudor king is delayed, because his army is suddenly stricken by a strange disease called the English Sweat. The terrible stench of their sweat is worse than the stink of war.

You are welcome to tickle Henry VIII's tongue or scratch his feet. But beware – from inside his whiffy sock drops his diseased big toe. It's finally rotted away and fallen off.

Scratch and sniff for a sweaty whiff!

Poor old Elizabeth I. Her gums rotted and her teeth went black, from eating too much sugar. She stuffed rags into her foul mouth to puff up her cheeks, hoping that no-one would notice the rot (unfortunately, her bad breath gave it away). Her favourite hair gel was made from apples and puppy fat, and her favourite perfume was lavender.

The Stench of War ~

The stench of war was certainly one of the most revolting aspects of smelly old history. In Tudor times, the Spanish Armada was a grisly affair. In 1588 King Philip II of Spain sent his fleet, or 'Armada', of Spanish galleons to fight the English, who had been annoying him by stealing his looted treasure in America, helping his enemies in Holland and ill-treating Catholics in England.

Although the defeat of the Armada was a great victory for the English navy, just imagine what life must have smelt like for the sailors on board ship. They were violently seasick, and the decks were often awash with vomit and crawling with rats.

Worst of all was the lowest deck, which was drenched with blood. This was where the ships' surgeon worked, amputating wounded limbs. The floors might be painted red – to disguise the blood. But nothing could disguise the smells of open surgery and reeking wounds. The barber-surgeon had dirty instruments and no antiseptic, so many wounds went septic and stank. However, you might be lucky if the maggots from the ship's biscuits crawled onto your wound and ate up all the bad bits of gangrene.

𝒜 Plague of Smells

The black rats and their fleas enjoy themselves in the streets of London, sizzling with the most wonderful smells of muck, dung and manure. The people are overpowered by the unbearable stench.

Plague was the most dreaded disease of Tudor times. Many people believed that it was bad smells, or miasmas, that carried the plague. They tried to protect themselves by smelling sweet herbs and flowers. Follow this story and see if you can sniff out the truth.

Evil Stinker is the enemy of the Tudor world. Today he is mixing up a plague potion for the rats of Stinking Street.

As Evil Stinker fires his plague potion, the rats fall down sick and dying of the plague.

The tiny fleas are hopping mad. With no rats to feed on, they must find new blood. Mistress Sickly proves a tasty morsel.

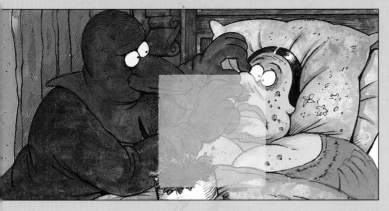

Poor Mistress Sickly is sick of the plague. The good Doctor Quack stuffs lavender and herbs up her nose. But it's too late.
Scratch the panel for a whiff of his hopeless remedy.

The plague explodes through the town. Evil Stinker chuckles and admires his work.

Doctor Quack can do nothing to save the sick townsfolk. But as a doctor it is important he saves his own life. He joins the fleeing throng.

Doctor Quack flees to the village of Pratt's Bottom until the plague is over in London. One family of rats, and their fleas, have also escaped. But Baby Ratty dies from the plague, and so his fleas hop onto Doctor Quack. Guess what happens next!!

15

Poxes and Posies

The plague was really vile, but there were many other awful poxes and pestilences in Tudor times. Catching a spotty pox was no laughing matter. Many people died from the Great Pox, smallpox, chickenpox and spotted fever. People carried 'roses and a pocketful of posies', to ward off the diseases. But other Tudor remedies were much less aromatic!

It could be dangerous to go for a haircut. Barbers also did minor (brutal) surgery, and pulled out teeth. This one's just removed a mouldy toe. Their red and white poles outside represented the blood and bandages of their trade!

This is the trial of Rowland Jenks in Oxford in 1577. He's going to have his ears cut off for not going to church. The courtroom is covered in aromatic herbs to cover up the awful smell of the prisoners and to protect people from their diseases, but it doesn't work. The prisoners gave everybody a lousy disease called typhus, which spread through the city, killing many people. It was spread by body lice, which loved their sweaty woollen clothes, but sadly no-one knew that.

Tudor doctors loved to remove foul and poisonous humours from the blood. This woman is having a 'phlebotomy', or blood-letting, for a boil – she's having blood removed by slimy black leeches on her back. Doctors also thought they could find out what was wrong with you by peering at your urine.

Odorous Occupations

There were lots of wonderfully stinky occupations to choose from in Tudor times:

Scavenger and Raker

Rake up heaps of manure and dung from the filthiest and foulest streets of London, throw it on your dung cart, dump it anywhere you like and come back for more.

Butcher and Fishmonger

Sell as much rotten meat and fish as you can for the highest price. But remember the rules: don't throw dead animals (or bits) into the river; don't leave old bones in the market place; don't sell fowl that's totally foul; carry your slops into the next town.

Scratch and sniff for a fishy reminder of a rotten occupation.

Ratcatcher

Catch grisly black rats, mice, polecats, weasels and moles.

Clapperdudgeon (a pretend beggar)

Cover yourself in loathsome running sores using ratsbane and arsenic, put on some filthy rags, slosh on some blood, limp from market to market begging for money, food and drink. Remember to remove it all at night when no-one is looking.

Candle-maker

Make candles all day in a stuffy workshop. This may sound like a bright and cheerful occupation, but it was one of the smelliest jobs of Tudor Britain. The candles were made from tallow (animal grease), which smelt absolutely foul.

Witch

If you don't fancy any of these, you could always be a witch. Witches were believed to come in all shapes and smells – old women with horrible warts, or women smelling of sulphur or rotten eggs. To see if you really were a witch you might be immersed in water. If you floated, you were guilty and therefore hanged. If you drowned, you were innocent!

Lousy Leisure

If you had any free time from your odorous occupation, there were plenty of lousy leisure activities to enjoy. Some were brutal and dangerous. In wrestling matches the aim was to break each other's bones. In cudgel play you hit your opponent on the head with a stick. The first one to draw blood was the winner. Other cruel events like bear-baiting and cock-fighting took place in cock-pits, where people crammed together to watch dogs attack chained-up bears, or birds fight each other to the death.

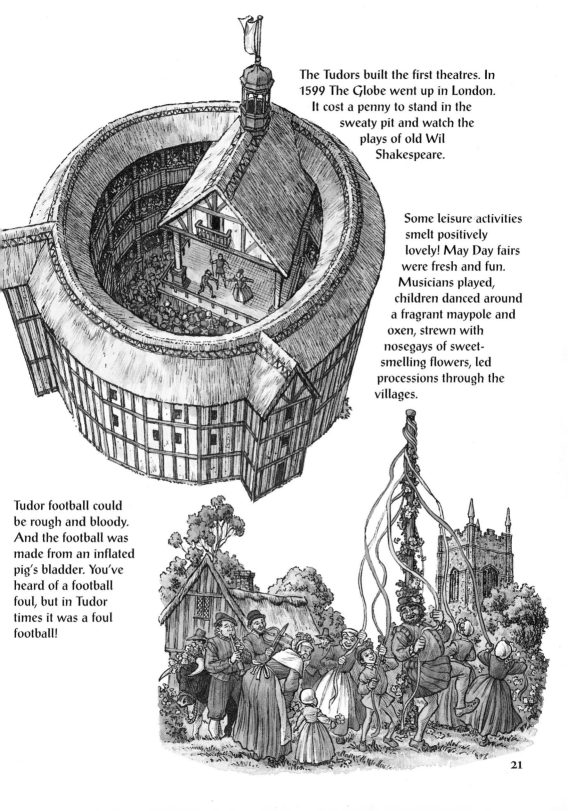

The Tudors built the first theatres. In 1599 The Globe went up in London. It cost a penny to stand in the sweaty pit and watch the plays of old Wil Shakespeare.

Some leisure activities smelt positively lovely! May Day fairs were fresh and fun. Musicians played, children danced around a fragrant maypole and oxen, strewn with nosegays of sweet-smelling flowers, led processions through the villages.

Tudor football could be rough and bloody. And the football was made from an inflated pig's bladder. You've heard of a football foul, but in Tudor times it was a foul football!

21

Appetising Aromas

Perfumed Peacocks · Violets in vinegary venison · Roast roses and beef

Mealtimes in Tudor Britain could be amazingly aromatic and exotic - for the lucky few. The rich really knew how to feast, as you can see below. For the poor, however, food could be hard to find and pretty uninteresting. But whether you were rich or poor, it was difficult to stop your food from going off. There were no fridges or freezers, so meat, fish, fruit and vegetables turned putrid very quickly. Fancy maggoty roast beef with mouldy bread, washed down with sour milk!

A really lavish Tudor dinner could be a deliciously (and disgustingly) smelly occasion. It might start at 10 o'clock in the morning and take several hours

Children's Menu: Mouldy porridge and Unsalted cabbage

The vast kitchens in the great manor houses had huge fireplaces roasting dozens of pigs, sheep and birds at a time. But together with the rich aromas of roasting came the stinks of rotting food and of the animals waiting to be slaughtered, not to mention a dozen sweaty cooks!

But the Tudors came up with lots of clever – and smelly – ideas to hide the rot. Salt was used to preserve food. Strong herbs from the garden and spices brought from overseas were thrown into the pot to disguise the decay. Even perfumes were added for extra fragrance.

Scratch and sniff the food on the table
for a spicy reminder of Tudor cooking.

Pickled Pigeons

Guinea ~~Fowl~~ Foul

Lark's Tongue in Lavender

Salted Swan

Garlic Cheese with cloves

Aromatic apple pie

Perfumed Palaces ～

The rich and famous of Tudor times really tried to make their sumptuous houses deliciously smelly, especially if the king or queen was coming to stay. Bess of Hardwick often had Elizabeth I, and all her courtiers, to stay at Hardwick Hall, which she made into a real perfumed palace.

The floors are sprinkled with sweet herbs and flowers from the beautiful gardens. The fragrant aroma of rosemary, lavender, thyme and rose drenches everything . Everybody's splendid clothes stink of rich perfumes. The scent from ambergris – the excretions of the sperm whale – is one of the best. Even the dogs are scented!

But underneath, the rushes on the floor are encrusted with animal and human filth. They're only replaced once a year!

Two sweethearts are exchanging their 'love apples', which they have kept in their armpits until saturated with sweat. To sniff the apple was a token of love!

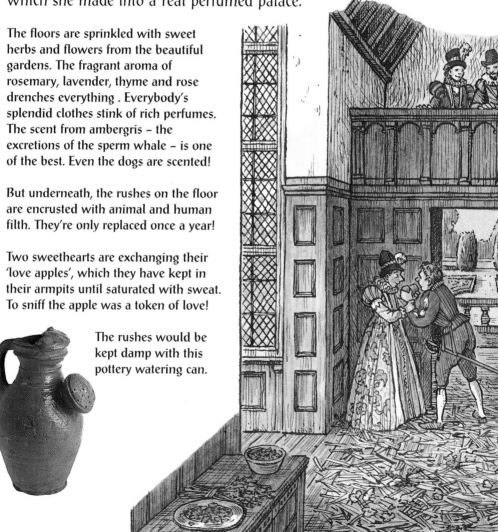

The rushes would be kept damp with this pottery watering can.

The bedchamber's pretty overpowering too. Flowers and nosegays are in every corner. Lavender has been pressed between the linen to perfume the sheets and to keep away illness. Just as well – the sheets are only washed every few months. The soap is made of whale fat soaked in rose water.

The Relief of the Poor . . .

The most common Tudor toilet was the chamber pot. The problem with this humble little pot was where to empty it. Sadly for Tudor citizens, this was usually out of the window, onto the passers-by. Or there was always the open fireplace – a smellier alternative, which might also put out the fire.

GARDEZ L'EAU!

Imagine how it must have been
To dress in finery all clean,
Then walk along the smelly street
With muck and filth about your feet.
Imagine too – an awful thought –
You're out there in your newly bought
Starchy ruff so fine and fair,
To make the passers-by all stare,
When trouping down the Strand one day
A noxious odour wafts your way.
You hear a cry, 'Please gardez l'eau',
But oh, too late for you to know!
Your ruff begins to drip and smell,
Your lovely clothes are ruined as well.
You look up, whereupon you spot
A lady with her chamber pot.
She smiles so sweetly from on high –
And tips another from the sky!

. . . and the Rich⁓

Royalty and the rich had softer options, as you can see below.

Some reeking royals tried to hide their chamber pots in fancy chairs. Henry VIII used a close stool like this one in Hampton Court Palace. To use it he was accompanied by the Yeoman of the Stool. Although it looks beautifully soft on the outside, you wouldn't want to take a close look inside.

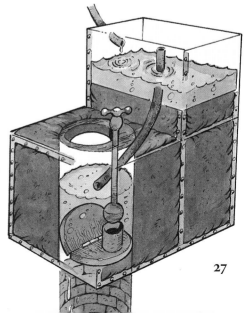

Elizabeth I had a highly sensitive nose, and was particularly concerned about this delicate problem. Her courtier and godson, Sir John Harington, invented for her the first flushing lavatory, which he called 'Ajax'. Bessie installed it in her palace at Richmond, and was said to be 'well-disposed' to it.

Spices, Smoke and Scurvy Knaves ⌣

This was the great age of exploration by sea. The smells of Old England were spread far and wide, and lots of new smells were brought wafting our way. Christopher Columbus sailed from Spain in search of spicy Asia. As we know, he took a wrong turn and discovered America instead. That was why Sir Walter Raleigh was able to bring from there new whiffs of tobacco smoke for the British people. Smoking a pipe was a fashionable way of fumigating the air to 'prevent' the plague.

Exotic spices

Raleigh enjoyed a pipe, but not everyone was used to this latest habit.

You might think that life on the ocean wave was as healthy as could be. But in fact the sailors had a rough and rotten time. Their cramped ships reeked of all the very worst Tudor odours.

Sailors were wretched scurvy knaves. Scurvy was a disease caused by eating too much salty meat, too many maggoty biscuits, and not enough fruit and green veggies. Scurvy caused horrible purple bleeding gums, rancid breath, putrid sores and black spotted legs. Sailors even tried washing out their mouths with urine as a cure. Eventually their teeth dropped out and they dropped down dead. Scurvy was the Black Death of the sea. So much for the healthy life . . .

Pungent Puzzles ～

Read the poem and fill in the smelly gaps.

The Tudors, we sense, were thoroughly rotten,
From nose to toe and head to ....
Their dunghills and muckheaps were piled so high,
Their ...... could be smelt from the ground to the sky.

When plague and disease presented a threat,
The king and queen and all subjects did ....
The doctors believed that their ...... were impure,
And offered some ......-smelling herbs as a cure.

All houses and churches were drenched in the stuff.
The rich sloshed it on from their gloves to their ruff.
But fragrant or ......, these smells scarce did the trick,
And people with pestilence died or were ....

With hindsight today, we can understand what
Those Tudors threw out with their foul chamber pot.
It was bugs, not the ...... , that led to disease,
And plague was transmitted by rats and their ....

Have a go at these Tudor teasers:

1. One Tudor writer thought plague may come by 'some stinking doonghills, filthie and standing pooles of water and unsavery smells.' Another thought it was because children were disobedient. What do you think?

2. Doctor Quack was a duck in disguise. True or false?

3. What is phlebotomy? a) the study of fleas b) a flabby bottom c) the removal of foul blood from the body?

Glossary

Ajax	the name given to the first flushing toilet.
barber-surgeon	a person who performed minor surgery on patients, as well as cutting their hair.
clapperdudgeon	a beggar who pretended to be diseased and injured.
close stool	a chair or stool with a built-in chamber pot, used as a toilet.
gangrene	the rotting of part of the body, when the blood supply has been cut off.
humours	the four substances in the body, which had to be kept in balance: black bile, yellow bile, blood and phlegm.
miasmas	bad odours in the air, believed to cause disease.
nosegay	a sweet-scented posy of flowers.
phlebotomy	the removal of foul blood from the body.
plague	a foul and deadly disease spread to people by bites from fleas that have bitten infected rats.
pomander	a decorated ball containing a mixture of aromatic herbs and spices, carried as a protection against infection.
pox	a disease causing a severe skin rash, such as chickenpox and smallpox.
quack	a fake doctor.
raker	a person who raked up the filth in the streets.
saltpetre	a substance used for making gunpowder.
scurvy	a disease caused by not eating enough fruit and vegetables.
typhus	a disease carried by body lice.

Index